JOHN NEWBERY

Publishing Pioneers

JOHN NEWBERY

FATHER OF CHILDREN'S LITERATURE

Marion Carnegie Library
206 S. Market St
Marion, IL 62959

by **Shirley Granahan**

Content Consultant:
Jill P. May
Professor of Literacy and Language, Purdue University

ABDO
Publishing Company

CREDITS

Published by ABDO Publishing Company, 8000 West 78th Street, Edina, Minnesota 55439. Copyright © 2010 by Abdo Consulting Group, Inc. International copyrights reserved in all countries. No part of this book may be reproduced in any form without written permission from the publisher. The Essential Library™ is a trademark and logo of ABDO Publishing Company.

Printed in the United States.

PRINTED ON RECYCLED PAPER

Editor: Holly Saari
Copy Editor: Paula Lewis
Interior Design and Production: Nicole Brecke
Cover Design: Nicole Brecke

Library of Congress Cataloging-in-Publication Data
Granahan, Shirley.
 John Newbery : father of children's literature / by Shirley Granahan.
     p. cm. — (Publishing pioneers)
 Includes bibliographical references and index.
 ISBN 978-1-60453-764-2
 1. Newbery, John, 1713-1767—Juvenile literature. 2. Publishers and publishing—England—Biography—Juvenile literature.
3. Children's literature—Publishing—England—History—18th century. 4. Newbery Medal—History—Juvenile literature. I. Title.

Z325.N53G73 2009
070.5092—dc22
 [B]

                         2009009993

TABLE OF CONTENTS

Before John Newbery began publishing children's books, children rarely read for fun.

BOOKS FOR CHILDREN

In 1744, English writer and publisher John Newbery did something that changed books and readership forever. At his London bookshop, he began to sell an illustrated book he had written especially for children's entertainment.

Prior to this, books for children had focused on education or instruction. Newbery's book was educational, but it was also fun to read. As a child, Newbery loved to read, but soon he discovered he had to borrow adult books to find anything entertaining. By writing his own book, Newbery would give children something to read that would teach and entertain them at the same time.

THE BOOK

Newbery's illustrated book, *A Little Pretty Pocket-Book*, was a compilation of rhymes about children's games written in alphabetical order. The text also described the rewards for being good and the punishments for being bad. The frontispiece had a motto in Latin, *Deluctando monemus,* "Instruction with Delight." This was the rhyme for the letter *B*:

Base-Ball.
The Ball once struck off,
Away flies the Boy
To the next destin'd Post,
And then Home with Joy.[1]

Below each rhyme was a moral, or lesson.

Thus Britons for Lucre [money]
Fly over the Main;

But, with Pleasure transported,

Return back again. [2]

The moral for the *B* rhyme implies that even if English citizens go to another country to make money, they are happiest when they return to England.

The book was small enough to fit in a pocket, and its cover and page edges were gilded, or golden. Most children had not seen this type of book before. The illustrations were inked from woodcarvings and were intriguing. Best of all, the characters in the book were ordinary children, not saints such as the characters in the prevalent religious stories of the time. Newbery offered the book to the public, and the public loved it. The book sold thousands of copies during and after Newbery's life.

THE AD MAN

Newbery's first children's book sold well, so he published more.

The Origins of *Baseball*

The word *baseball* has been dated to 1744 and Newbery. In *A Little Pretty Pocket-Book,* the word is used in the *B* rhyme. An illustration shows boys playing the game, but instead of the bags and home plate that are familiar today, the bases are posts.

BASE-BALL.

THE *Ball* once ftruck off,
        Away flies the *Boy*
To the next deftin'd Poft,
And then Home with Joy.

The B rhyme in A Little Pretty Pocket-Book

He wrote some books himself. He also hired well-known authors to write the works.

Before long, Newbery was famous in London as a friend to children. He reminded potential buyers of his friendly, uncle-like attitude in an announcement in the *London Chronicle*:

The Philosophers, Politicians . . . and the learned in every faculty are desired to observe that on the first of January, being New Year's day, . . . Mr Newbery intends to publish the following important volumes, bound and gilt, and hereby invites all his little friends who are good to call for them at the Bible and Sun in St. Paul's Churchyard, but those who are naughty to have none.[3]

Newbery had proved that children's publishing was profitable. It also became an important branch of literature. Newbery was committed to making children's reading material fun—making a profit at the same time was a bonus.

As Margaret Kinnell explained in *Children's Literature: An Illustrated History*, few people have been as instrumental as Newbery in popularizing children's literature. Kinnel wrote,

John Newbery has often been credited with originating the publication of children's

Character in a Book

Irish author Oliver Goldsmith was a friend of Newbery. In Goldsmith's novel, *The Vicar of Wakefield,* he included a Newbery-like character. He described the character: "This person was the philanthropic bookseller in St. Paul's Churchyard, who has written so many little books for children: he called himself their friend, but he was the friend of all mankind."[4]

books; in reality, though, his role was even more important: he began the serious business of publishing for children.[5]

As an advertising man, Newbery was a genius. He ran the following newspaper ad for his first book in the *Penny Morning Post* on June 13, 1744:

A Little Pretty Pocket-Book, intended for the Instruction and Amusement of Little Master Tommy and Pretty Miss Polly . . . will infallibly make Tommy a good Boy and Polly a Good Girl.[6]

To ensure he reached those who would actually buy the book, Newbery made sure his books

The Right to Print

Many of Newbery's books were published "by the King's authority," the way in which copyright was given at that time. One of the official announcements stated,

GEORGE the Second, by the Grace of God, King of Great Britain, . . . to all whom these presents shall concern, Greeting. Whereas our trusty and well-beloved John Newbery of London, Bookseller, hath, with great expence and much labour, compiled a work intitled 'The Circle of the Sciences; or, The Compendious Library,' digested in a method entirely new, whereby each branch of Polite Literature is rendered extremely easy and instructive. We being willing to encourage all works of public benefit, are graciously pleased to grant him our royal privilege and licence for the sole printing, publishing, and vending the same.

Given at St James', the 8th of December 1744, by His Majesty's Command,

Holles Newcastle.[7]

included instructions for parents. Inside the books, he included a letter to parents, guardians, and other caretakers in which he gave hints on helping their children grow up healthy, wise, virtuous, and happy.

Cross-referencing

A shrewd businessman, Newbery was never shy about advertising his other products in his books. He would often mention himself and his company in the text of books he published. In one such book, a child laments to his father about the not-so-lucky children:

> *My dear papa, I cannot help pitying those poor little boys whose parents are not in a condition to purchase them such a nice gilded library as that with which you have supplied me from my good friends at the corner of St Paul's Churchyard. Surely such unhappy boys must be very ignorant all their lives, for what can they learn without books.* [8]

Newbery also used *A Little Pretty Pocket-Book* to advertise his publishing company. In one part of the book, a character sings a song, and the text describes where the lyrics can be found: "She then sung the 'Cuzz's Chorus' (which may be found in the 'Little Pretty Plaything' published by Mr Newbery)." [9]

Newbery used clever newspaper advertisements for his books.

Toys for Good Girls and Boys

Newbery was a pioneer in pairing children's books with accessories. *A Little Pretty Pocket-Book* was advertised as follows: "Price of Book alone, 6 [pennies], with a Ball or Pincushion, 8 [pennies]."[10] Customers likely found the accessory worth the few extra pennies. The ball was meant for a boy and the pincushion for a girl, since most girls during that time learned to sew.

Although the concept of kindergartens did not exist until the 1830s, Newbery created a product for

Incentive to Be Good?

In Newbery's time, most little girls learned to sew. Newbery knew this and used the cushions as a way to "make Polly a good girl." Each pin-cushion was half-red and half-black. If the child was good, a pin was put in the red half. If she did something naughty, a pin was put in the black half.

preschoolers. It was a set of cutout blocks to help children learn to spell and do math.

Newbery became so well known for his innovations in children's literature that a special award was named after him. Every year, the Newbery Medal is awarded for the best children's book written in the United States. In many ways, Newbery's legacy still influences children's literature. ⌐

Newbery contributed many books to the genre of children's literature.

Newbery grew up on a small farm in rural England.

A Country Boy

John Newbery was born in Waltham St. Lawrence, England, in July 1713. He was the second son of farmer Robert Newbery. Not a lot is known about John Newbery's childhood, but as was common for farm children of that time, he and his older brother Robert likely helped with the many chores required for growing crops and raising livestock. And like most farm boys, Robert and John were probably expected to become farmers when they grew up.

While Robert was interested in becoming a farmer, John was not. He was more interested in other things, including a career path that an ancestor had already traveled. Ralph Newbery had been a London publisher in the late 1500s and early 1600s. Although John was born more than a century after Ralph Newbery, John would follow in his ancestor's footsteps in the publishing industry.

Lessons and Learning

John attended the village school and was taught the basics—reading, writing, and a bit of math. These types of skills were thought necessary to become a farmer. Children of all ages were taught in one school

Waltham St. Lawrence

Waltham St. Lawrence is a small country village with a population of approximately 1,000. A lot of farmland remains, but many residents work in nearby towns, such as Reading, or commute to London. The village still has a picturesque quality of an old-world community. A part-time post office, a gas station, and two public houses, or inns, do business there. The village has one church—portions of which date back 850 years—which the Newberys most likely attended.

and by one teacher. Quite often, bright children were made assistant teachers or monitors. It is likely that John was one of these assistants in the Waltham St. Lawrence village school. Years later, Francis Newbery, John's son, wrote in his autobiography about his father: "by his talents and industry, and a great love of books, [John] had rendered himself a very good English scholar."[1]

When John was a boy, many families did not own books other than a Bible. Books were expensive. Farmers usually did not have much money and sometimes found it difficult to meet their basic needs.

A Chip Off the Old Block

Ralph Newbery, like his descendant John, was born on a farm in Waltham St. Lawrence. Ralph left the farm and headed for the big city of London, where he made his mark as a printer and a publisher. Ralph concentrated on producing adult reading materials. He rose to become master of the Royal Printing House of Queen Elizabeth I and her successor, King James I.

Ralph printed his first book, *Pallengenius*, in 1600. His name appears on many of the important books published during his lifetime, including Raphael Holinshed's *Chronicles of England, Scotland, and Ireland*, which relates the histories of the three countries. The publication is believed to be Shakespeare's major source for his English history plays and *King Lear, Macbeth,* and *Cymbeline*. Ralph retired in 1605.

Upon his death in 1608, he left a house and land in Waltham St. Lawrence for the benefit of the poor and needy of the village. The house, which became the Bell Inn, still stands by the local church and graveyard where Ralph is buried.

They could not afford the luxury of books. However, a wealthy landowner or a minister from a well-to-do family could afford the popular books of the time, such as John Bunyan's *Pilgrim's Progress*, Daniel Defoe's *Robinson Crusoe*, and Jonathan Swift's *Gulliver's Travels*. Since John loved books and reading, he may have borrowed these books from other villagers who owned them.

The Country Boy Goes to Town

At age 16, John moved away from home to the nearby town of Reading. He became an apprentice to William Ayres, publisher of the *Reading Mercury* newspaper. When John arrived in Reading, he discovered it was quite different from his little village. Reading was on the road from London to Bristol where the Thames and Kennet rivers met. Farmers brought sheep, cattle, and grain to sell in the Reading market. People

Farming in the 1700s

In the early 1700s, village land was split into three or four large open fields divided into strips separated by land that was not plowed. Each villager farmed a number of strips in the fields. Crop rotation was necessary to replenish the soil. So, one field was left unsown each year. Fewer planted fields resulted in few leftover crops to use as winter feed for the animals. Many animals were slaughtered before winter because they would never survive otherwise without the extra feed.

By 1800, farmers began to put hedges or fences around individual farm fields. By doing this, farmers could farm their own land the way they wanted. More land was cultivated more efficiently. With more winter food available for animals, fewer were killed in autumn. That, in turn, meant more fresh meat available to villagers throughout the winter months.

An illustration of a scene in Gulliver's Travels

bustled through the market and along the roads. Barges filled the waterways of the town.

The newspaper office was a busy place, too. The small pressroom was filled with the tools of the printer's trade, including presses, boxes of type, and ink. The office held copies of the recent newspaper issues. John was eager to learn how they were printed. He discovered how to arrange the letters of type into backward words—as they would appear on the page in reverse. He learned how to lock the letters into an iron form called a chase and how to put the chase on the press. He learned to ink the form so that the words would print on the paper. The machine squeezed paper against inky letters to transfer their images. John learned to dry freshly inked pages by hanging them on the lines strung across the shop. When a print run was finished, he helped remove the type from the form, sorted the letters, and put them back in the box until he needed to compose another chase.

John worked hard to learn the skills of the printing trade. As Francis Newbery later wrote of his father:

> *His mind was too excursive to allow him to devote his life to the occupation of agriculture. He was anxious to be in trade, and at about the age of sixteen, as he was a very good accountant, and wrote an excellent hand, he engaged himself as an assistant in the house of*

The *Reading Mercury*

The first edition of the *Reading Mercury* came off the press on July 8, 1723. William Parks and David Kinnier started the newspaper in Berkshire County. For more than 250 years, the paper continued under other owners and publishers, including William Ayres and William Carnan. It is likely that the paper had a large circulation.

Learning a Trade

To become an apprentice, a boy moved away from his home and family and moved into the home of a master tradesman, such as a printer, a blacksmith, a silversmith, or a furniture maker. The master provided lodging, food, clothing, and on-the-job training so that when the apprenticeship was over, the boy would be able to earn a living at the trade. While in the master's house, the boy was generally treated like one of the family and had to follow all family rules. A normal apprenticeship lasted approximately three years, though it could range from one to six years.

one of the principal merchants in Reading, where his diligence and integrity soon established his character, while his agreeable manners and conversation, and information (for he pursued his studies in all his leisure hours) raised him into notice and esteem. [2]

Due to his hard work and skill, John soon became the assistant to printer William Carnan, a man who would start him on a groundbreaking career in publishing.

*At age 16, Newbery traveled from Waltham St. Lawrence to Reading
to become an apprentice.*

Chapter 3

A master and his apprentice work on a printing press.

TAKING CARE OF BUSINESS

William Ayres ran the *Reading Mercury* when Newbery became his apprentice in 1730. A few years later, William Carnan took over. He kept Newbery on staff and continued to train him.

Along with publishing the weekly *Reading Mercury,* Carnan was a merchant at his shop, the Bible and Crown. He sold medicines and various other goods. Newbery learned this business, too, and most likely put his bookkeeping skills to good use by monitoring the accounts at the country store.

Newbery also may have used his bookkeeping skills to keep track of taxes owed to the government. Like most newspapers, the *Reading Mercury* ran ads for local merchants who paid the paper to advertise their businesses. The more ads a paper printed, the more money the publisher made. As newspaper advertising increased, the British government wanted a share of the profits. In 1712, Parliament passed the Stamp Act. This imposed a tax on "every Advertisement to be contained in the *London Gazette,* or any other printed Paper, such Paper being dispersed or made publick Weekly, or oftener."[1]

Newbery and Carnan worked side-by-side for almost seven years.

Books to Share

In the early 1740s, Newbery set up the Newbery Circulating Library in Reading so that those who could not afford to buy books could still have access to them. It was not until the late nineteenth century that the British public library system became well established.

Throughout this time, Newbery lived with Carnan, Carnan's wife, Mary, and their three children. He was treated as a family member. Near the end of 1737, William Carnan died. He bequeathed his property and business to his brother Charles and to Newbery.

A New Family

Upon the death of her husband, Mary Carnan ran the paper. At that time, most British women did not work outside the home. But after Carnan died, Mary was listed as publisher of the *Reading Mercury*. During that time, she and Newbery grew closer, and in 1739 they married. Mary must have been relieved to have someone who would provide for her and her children. When Carnan died, his three children— John, Thomas, and Anna Maria—were left without a father. Newbery took on the responsibility for supporting and raising the Carnan children.

Newbery was a good husband and stepfather. He worked hard to find new ways to make money for his family. He had grown up as an apprentice in the Carnan household, so Mary and the children knew him well and liked him.

At the newspaper, Newbery arranged movable type for the printing press.

Mary and Newbery eventually had three more children: Mary, John, and Francis. When John was a young boy, he fell down steps and badly hurt his spine. The family suffered a tragic loss when he died at the age of 11.

On the Road

After he married Mary, an ambitious Newbery took over running the newspaper and the shop. He took on a new partner, Charles Micklewright, at the newspaper. In 1740, Newbery went on the road to spread the word about the goods and services available at the Bible and Crown and to increase the shop's customer base.

On July 9, Newbery headed to London by stagecoach. He also visited many other towns around England. He kept an account of his trip in his journal, jotting down facts about each day's travel. These included how far he traveled, where he spent the night, and descriptions of towns, products, and sights of interest along the way.

Since machines were rare at the time, Newbery noted, "Going from Leicester to Coventry we pass by . . . two Engine Houses which are wrought by fire and throw a great quantity of water out of the pits."[2] What he saw were steam engines at a cotton mill. It was one signal that a new industrial world was taking shape.

One note in Newbery's journal told of his fascination with the "Ducking Stool." He discovered that some towns used it to punish wives.

Newbery's Notes

Newbery's notes hint at his personality and keen business sense. In his biography of Newbery, Charles Welsh quotes these passages from Newbery's journal: "Let Mr Micklewright print a *Reading Mercury and Advertiser* once a fortnight, and J. Carnan print a *Reading Mercury and Weekly Post* once a fortnight, and by that means save duty of advertisements. Note, let the titles be *The Reading Mercury* and *The Reading Courant*."[3]

The British government collected special taxes on weekly publications. Newbery understood that he could avoid paying this tax by setting up the newspaper under two different names. Each newspaper was printed every other week, so it did not have to pay the weekly tax.

Some women were tied to the stool and plunged underwater. This was supposed to prohibit them from becoming cranky wives. Newbery must have thought it was a good idea because he wrote, "A plan of this instrument I shall procure and transplant to Berkshire for the good of my native county."[4]

Newbery also bought, or at least noted the prices of, anything he thought he could sell in the Reading store, such as cutlery, haberdashery, medicines, books, and stationery. He bought new typefaces for the presses in Reading and listed books he wanted to publish on his press at the newspaper office. Newbery returned to Reading in August 1740 and began to carry out some of his ideas.

New Enterprises

With his new partner Micklewright, Newbery published his first books in 1740. One was a reprint of a book he made note of on his travels, clergyman Richard Allestree's *The Whole Duty of Man*. The book was a guide to religious behavior and cultural relations. The second book he published was Irish poet Samuel Boyse's *Miscellaneous Works for the Amusement of the Fair Sex*. The book was filled with text the author thought women would enjoy.

Newbery also opened a printing business, utilizing the presses even more. An ad in the *Reading Mercury* announced that printing services were now available from J. Newbery and C. Micklewright. The owners guaranteed that any work ordered would be completed in the neatest manner.

After his journey to London, Newbery opened a wholesale warehouse, selling haberdashery supplies such as thread, tape, binding, ribbon, pins, and needles to other shopkeepers. He advertised that his goods were as inexpensive as the goods sold in London. Customers could save the time, money, and inconvenience of taking the long trip to town, and Newbery and Micklewright could make a larger profit because of it. Newbery encouraged shopkeepers to write to him at the Bible and Crown and order supplies through a mail-order service.

READY REMEDIES

Newbery continued to sell popular medicines at the Bible and Crown. These included Daffy's Elixir and Greenough's Tincture for the Teeth. Thomas Daffy, inventor of the elixir, was a clergyman whose mixture was advertised as a cure for many ailments. Daffy's Elixir was created as a therapy for a cough or cold. However, advertisers such as Newbery often chose not to link a product with a specific ailment, hoping to appeal to a wider range of potential buyers.

Newbery expanded the medicine business and added products to his inventory. In 1743, he and three other shopkeepers paid Dr. John Hooper of Reading for the right to sell Hooper's "female pills" for 14 years in their shops.

TIME TO BRANCH OUT

The *Reading Mercury* thrived under Newbery's ownership. The book and medicine businesses were also doing well. A shrewd

Physicians' Concoctions

In the early days of modern medicine, scientists used a few effective herbal and mineral drugs. People wanted doctors to prescribe wonder drugs for their ailments. But a small number of tested remedies were not enough to cover all the problems for which people wanted treatment. Physicians and others began to make their own concoctions from various ingredients, including caraway seeds, raisins, licorice, and alcohol.

Many members of the British royalty used these elixirs. If a royal used a medicine and it worked, the inventor or manufacturer was issued a "letters patent," or "open letter," authorizing the use of the royal endorsement in advertising. However, the effectiveness of these elixirs was not scientifically proven. Some people were opposed to these medicinal concoctions and believed them to be phony products. One physician, Thomas Wakley, believed Daffy's Elixir was a fake medicine sold by unqualified people as a way to make money. Even with its critics, however, Daffy's Elixir remained on the market for 300 years.

businessman, Newbery saw more potential for these interests. In 1744, he opened a Bible and Crown shop in London. He left his stepson, John Carnan, in charge of the printing business in Reading. The business in London went so well that Newbery decided it was time for his family to move. In 1745, the Newbery family relocated to London. There, Newbery moved his shop to 65 St. Paul's Churchyard and renamed it the Bible and Sun. ⌐

THE
READING POST:
Or, WEEKLY MERCURY.

NUMB. 27

MONDAY, *DECEMBER* 21, 1730.   [Price 2 d.]

AN
ACCOUNT

Of The THRESHER'S LABOUR.

From Scrip and Bottle hope new Strength to gain ;
But Scrip and Bottle too are try'd in vain.
Down our parch'd Throats we scarce the Bread can get,
And quite o'er-spent with Toil, but faintly eat ;
Nor can the Bottle only answer all,
Alas ! the Bottle and the Beer's too small.
Our Time slipes on, we move from off the Grass,
And each again betakes him to his Place.
Not eager now, as late, our Strength to prove,
But all contented regular to move :
Often we whet, as often view the Sun,
To see how near his tedious Race is run ;
At length he vails his radiant Face from Sight,
And bids the weary Traveller good-night :
Homewards we move, but so much spent with Toil,
we walk but slow and rest at every Stile.
Our good expecting Wives, who think we stay,
Got to the Door, soon eye us to the way ;
Then from the Pot the Dumpling's catch'd in haste,
And homely by its side the Bacon's plac'd
Supper and Sleep by Morn new Strength supply,
And out we set again our Works to try :
But not so early quite, nor quite so fast,
As to our Cost we did the Morning past.
Soon as the rising Sun has drank the Dew,
Another Scene is open'd to our View ;
Our Mester comes, and at his Heels a Throng
Of prating Females, arm'd with Rake and Prong ;
Prepar'd, whilst he is here, to make his Hay ;
Or, if he turns his Back, prepar'd to play.
But here, or gone, sure of this Comfort still,
Here's Company, so they may chat their fill :
And were their Hands as Active as their Tongues,
How nimbly then would move their Rakes and Prongs ?
The Grass again is spread upon the Ground,
Till not a vacant Place is to be found ;
And while the piercing Sun-beams on it shine,
The Haymakers have time allow'd to dine :
That soon dispatch'd, they still sit on the Ground,
And the brisk Chat renew'd, a-fresh goes round :
All talk at once, but seeming all to fear,
That all they speak so well, the rest won't hear ;
By quick degrees so high their Notes they strain,
That Standers-by can nought distinguish'd plain :
So loud their Speech, and so confus'd their Noise,
Scarce puzzled Echo can return a Voice ;
Yet spite of this, they bravely all go on,
Each scorns to be, or seem to be, outdone ;
Till (unobserv'd before) a low'ring Sky,
Fraught with black Clouds, proclaims a Shower nigh ;

The tatling Croud can scarce their Garments gain,
Before descends the thick impetuous Rain :
Their noisy Prattle all at once is done,
And to the Hedge they all for Shelter run.

Thus have I seen on a bright Summer's Day,
On some green Brake a Flock of Sparrows play ;
From Twig to Twig, from Bush to Bush they fly,
And with continu'd Chirping fill the Sky ;
But on a sudden, if a Storm appears,
Their chirping Noise no longer dins your Ears ;
They fly for Shelter to the thickest Bush,
There silent fit, and all at once is hush.
But better Fate succeeds this rainy Day,
And little Labour serves to make the Hay ;
Fast as 'tis cut, so kindly shines the Sun,
Turn'd once or twice, the pleasing Work is done :
Next Day the Cocks appear in equal Rows,
Which the glad Master in safe Reeks bestows.

But now the Field we must no longer range,
And yet, hard Fate ! still Work for Work we change,
Back to the Barns again in haste we're sent,
Where lately so much Time we pensive spent ;
Not pensive now ; we bless the friendly Shade,
And to avoid the parching Sun are glad.
But few Days here we're distin'd to remain,
Before our Master calls us forth again :
For Harvest now, says he, yourselves prepare,
The ripen'd Harvest now demands your Care.
Early next Morn I shall disturb your Rest,
Get all things ready, and be quickly drest :
Strict to his Word, scarce the next Dawn appears,
Before his hasty Summons dills our Ears.
Obedient to his Call, strait up we get,
And finding soon our Company complete ;
With him, our Guide, we to the Wheat-Field go ;
He, to appoint, and we the Work, to do.
Ye Reapers, cast your Eyes around the Field,
And view the Scene its different Beauties yield :
Then look again with a more tender Eye,
To think how soon it must in Ruin lie.
For once set in, where e'er our Blows we deal,
There's no resisting of the well whet Steel :
But here or there, where e'er our Course we bend,
Sure Desolation does our Steps attend.
Thus, when *Arabia's* Sons, in hopes of Prey,
To some more fertile Country take their way ;
How beauteous all things in the Morn appear,
There Villages, and pleasing Cots are here ;
So many pleasing Objects meet the Sight,
The ravish'd Eye could willing gaze 'till Night :
But long e'er then, where-e'er their Troops have past,
Those pleasant Prospects lie a gloomy Waste.

The Morning past, we sweat beneath the Sun,
And but uneasily our Work goes on.
Before us we perplexing Thistles find,
And Corn blown adverse with the ruffling Wind ;
[*To be continu'd in my next.*]

The front page of a 1730 issue of the Reading Mercury

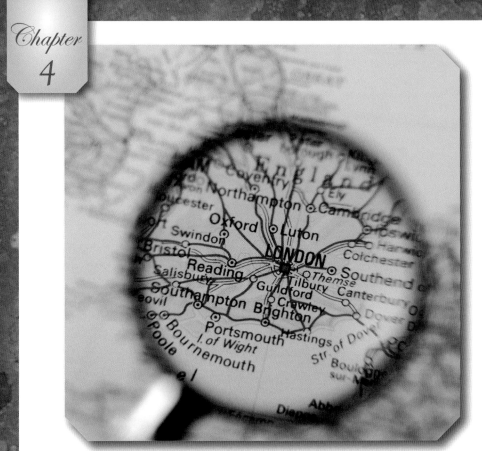

The Newberys moved from Reading to London in 1745.

OFF TO LONDON

The move from Reading to London was likely a big change for the Newbery family. Although Newbery had experienced quite a bit of London, his wife and his children had not. At that time, it was the largest city in Europe and had a population of more than 600,000 people.

The city was an animated, colorful, noisy place that could be both exciting and terrifying. The streets were paved with cobblestones. Wheels on coaches and wagons made a clattering sound as they rumbled over the bumpy streets, accompanied by the clip-clop of their horses' hooves. Merchants pushed carts along the streets, musically calling out what they had for sale and how much it cost. Throngs of people rushed by on their way to shops, and children played in narrow streets and alleyways. Heavy signs hanging outside shops on large metal bars were regularly battered by the wind. Sometimes, the weight of a swinging sign brought an entire front wall crashing down on the ground. As Newbery's friend, author Samuel Johnson, wrote, "Here falling Houses thunder on your Head . . . ."[1]

Pictures instead of Words

The symbols on signs hanging outside shops were designed for a specific reason. Not everyone was able to read in London in the mid-eighteenth century. Illiterate shoppers could locate a shop based on the pictures on the shop signs. A shop that sold musical instruments might have violin and harp pictures, and a shop that sold books might have an open book on its sign.

London business districts were often crowded in the eighteenth and nineteenth centuries.

At night, the men of the Watch walked the streets carrying lanterns and calling out the time.

In this port city, boats moved up and down the Thames River, bringing goods from around the world. Farmers who brought livestock to sell herded the animals down the streets toward waiting barges on the river.

In 1666, a great fire in London had consumed much of the city. Remaining buildings were patched and new buildings were constructed. The buildings were organized to have many people in a small area, which left narrow, unlit passageways between homes and shops. Many structures had crumbling bricks and faltering wooden beams.

London was a dirty city. Fresh country air did not fill the lanes as it had in Reading. Garbage and human waste collected on the streets. The smell was overwhelming. Most people kept their windows shut at all times. Water for city residents came from the murky waters of the Thames River through hollowed-out tree trunks running under the streets. But the Thames was polluted with garbage and waste that entered the river from the streets. Water was not filtered until the mid-nineteenth century.

St. Paul's Churchyard

The neighborhood of St. Paul's Churchyard encompasses all sides of the cathedral. In early times, it was just a yard surrounding the church, but over the years, the church acquired more land. A stone wall was built, with gates that were opened from dawn to night. For centuries, the churchyard was a central meeting place for public events. The first shops were built around 1587. Shops published and sold sheet music as well as musical instruments.

With its overpopulation, bad sanitation, and poor structures, London was a hotbed of bacteria and disease. Sickness and death were common, but Newbery felt that with the proper awareness and attention, his family and his businesses could thrive in the exciting, growing city. According to Samuel Johnson,

> "[Y]ou find no man, at all intellectual, who is willing to leave London. No, Sir, when a man is tired of London, he is tired of life; for there is in London all that life can afford."[2]

Extended Family

Newbery did not forget his family back in Waltham St. Lawrence, where his brother, Robert, had become a farmer. Robert's son, Francis, was more interested in publishing than in farming. Newbery took his nephew Francis in as an apprentice. Soon, Francis became an important part of the Newbery publishing company.

Newbery and his brother, Robert, kept in touch. Because of Newbery's medicine business, Robert and others assumed Newbery had a real knowledge of healing. In 1752, Newbery received letters from Robert and other farmers in Waltham

St. Lawrence asking what they should do about the horses and cattle in their area that were becoming sick. The answer Newbery gave the farmers was never documented. However, it is known that he left London for a time and later received many letters revealing that a medicine called Dr. James's Fever Powder was used for the sick animals.

THE FAMILY HOME

The Newberys moved into their new home in St. Paul's Churchyard in 1744. Not much is known about their family life there, but it might have been similar to the lives of other shop owners who lived in comfortable quarters above their stores. Other shops and restaurants

St. Paul's Cathedral

The original St. Paul's Cathedral in London was a wooden structure built in 604. It was destroyed by a fire in 675, rebuilt, burned again in 1087, and again rebuilt by 1214. It is the third-longest church in Europe at 596 feet (182 m).

In 1666, the Great Fire engulfed the city. Flames spread through London's closely packed streets and predominantly wooden structures, destroying two-thirds of the city. Hot lead from the melting bells and dome of St. Paul's Cathedral poured down on the pavement, making it too dangerous for any help to get close. Four days later, St. Paul's Cathedral was a pile of rubble. Once again, it was rebuilt. The first stone was laid on June 21, 1675, and 22 years later, the new church opened. It includes the whispering gallery—a circular walkway halfway up the inside of the dome. A person who whispers by one wall can be heard clearly by someone standing near the opposite wall.

A London residence in the eighteenth century

were nearby, as well as a play area near St. Paul's
Cathedral. The busy neighborhood, known as St.
Paul's Churchyard, was home to many vendors,
including book and music shops. These may have
offered adults opportunities for friendly get-
togethers.

In 1760, the Newberys moved into Canonbury House. The building in London's central borough of Islington was constructed in the fourteenth century and had been home to many poets and political leaders. According to Newbery's son Francis, Oliver Goldsmith once lived there and read Francis parts of his poems, including a ballad from *The Vicar of Wakefield*.

As Newbery believed in keeping his businesses in the family, his sons, nephew, and stepsons helped him at the newspaper and the shop. He taught them all he could about the businesses Carnan had started and that Newbery himself had built up.

Thomas Carnan became his stepfather's right-hand man in the shop. John Carnan took to the combination of publishing and selling, like his father and stepfather. When Newbery and his family moved to London, Newbery left the

Family Tradition

Newbery's daughter, Mary, married Michael Power, a Spanish merchant, in 1766. They had a large family, some of whom were later linked to Newbery's London bookshop. In the late 1780s, Mary's son, Francis Power, published a few books from 65 St. Paul's Churchyard, emphasizing that he was Newbery's grandson.

A Stepdaughter Marries

In 1752, Anna Maria Carnan married poet and songwriter Christopher Smart. They had two daughters, Marianne and Elizabeth Anne. Smart was known for his reckless spending habits and was arrested for debt in 1747. Newbery gave him a job and helped support his house and family, but, unfortunately, Smart suffered a mental breakdown. While confined in an asylum, Smart wrote *A Song to David,* believed to be his best work. *Hymns for the Amusement of Children* was his last known work. He was arrested again for debt in 1770 and died in prison the following year.

Reading shop in the capable hands of his eldest stepson, John. In 1762, Newbery put his stepdaughter Anna Maria in charge of the *Reading Mercury*. Newbery's businesses would continue to thrive with their contributions.

St. Paul's Cathedral in London

Newbery's publishing business gave children entertaining books to read.

CHILDREN'S LITERATURE
BEFORE NEWBERY

After Newbery and his family were settled in London, he emerged as a famed writer and publisher of entertaining, educational books for children. Before Newbery published *A Little Pretty Pocket-Book* in 1744, children's books were not an important category of literature. C. M. Hewins wrote in "The History of Children's Books" for the *Atlantic Monthly,* "There have been children's stories and folk-tales ever since man first learned to speak. Children's books, however, are a late growth of literature."[1]

Children's literature includes any text written expressly for children, as well as materials children choose to read on their own. Because of this, the distinction between children's literature and adult literature can become unclear. Before Newbery, people often thought some material meant specifically for adults could be considered children's literature because children read the stories. These included ancient myths, folktales, and fables that attempted to explain natural phenomena, such as the changing of the seasons and why there is night and day.

Storytellers passed these narratives down from generation to generation by word of mouth, and eventually some stories made it into print. However, at that time, most children could not read. Those who could read found the language and length of any available books difficult. The subject matter was not meant specifically for them either.

Johannes Gutenberg invented the printing press in the mid-fifteenth century.

In the Middle Ages, texts designed for children consisted of rhymes about manners that were for educating, not entertaining. During this time, books were handwritten. It was a time-consuming task to produce copies of a book by hand. In the mid-fifteenth century, Johannes Gutenberg invented the movable-type printing press. This invention allowed publishers to print numerous copies of a book in a short period of time. The printing press saved both time and money because more books were printed in less time. With more reading material available, more people learned to read.

MORE READERS, MORE READING MATERIAL

Several new types of reading materials emerged in the sixteenth century: hornbooks, broadsides, and chapbooks. Hornbooks were a kind of primer, or first reader, for schoolchildren. Information to be learned, such as the alphabet, numbers, a rhyme, and the Lord's Prayer, was printed on one side of a sheet of parchment. A transparent layer of an animal's horn was placed over the paper to protect it from dirty hands and moisture. The two sheets were then attached to a wooden paddle that had a handle, making it easy for a child to hold and carry from place to place.

The Printing Press

In the mid-fifteenth century, Johannes Gutenberg fashioned a new metal alloy from which to cast letters for setting type. The separate pieces of type could be used and reused by rearranging them to spell new words. This lowered the price of printed materials, making them available to more people. Gutenberg's printing press helped the advancement of science, art, and religion through the communication of ideas in texts. The Gutenberg technique was the standard in printing until the twentieth century.

A chapbook of Robinson Crusoe

A broadside was a large sheet of paper with printing on one side that usually included a woodcut illustration and a line or so of text. The picture would align with the text, so the meaning of the text could be inferred from the picture. Often, a broadside was hung on a wall, so it served a similar purpose to a poster and conveyed a visual message.

Chapbooks were small, cheaply made books that usually had between 8 and 32 pages. The books were filled with jokes, recipes, and short stories that often came from local folklore. Chapbooks were quite cheap, so even the less wealthy could afford to buy and enjoy them. They may have been designed for adults, but children enjoyed reading them as well.

CHANGING THE MARKET

During the seventeeth century, the deep-rooted faith of Puritans required them to be literate so they could read and understand the Bible. Children needed to be able to read for these reasons as well.

Puritans created many children's books designed to provide religious and moral instruction. The books were often filled with lessons because the adults believed books were meant to teach a child. A child's mind was considered something that needed to be improved. Imagination was discouraged and reality of life was stressed, especially the religious and moral aspects.

Chapbooks

Peddlers known as chapmen sold chapbooks. *Chap* is an Old English word for *trade*. So, a chapman was a tradesman who sold books. Chapmen sold their wares on street corners in the city or along roads while traveling through the countryside. Chapbooks usually contained between 8 and 32 pages, with text that included folklore and religious instruction. Books sold for two to three pence, or pennies.

Material specifically for children was published as early as 1576. These materials consisted of primers, histories, and hymnbooks that focused on faith and knowledge. One exception to the rule was a chapbook with a very long title, about a very small creature, called *The History of Tom Thumbe, the Little, for his small stature surnamed, King Arthurs Dwarfe: Whose Life and adventures containe many strange and wonderful accidents, published for the delight of merry Time-spenders.* Written by Richard Johnson, the book was published in England in 1621. It was an entertaining story enjoyed by adults and children.

In 1671, a Puritan preacher and writer, James Janeway, published *A Token for Children: Being an Exact Account of the Conversion, Holy and Exemplary Lives and Joyful Deaths of Several Young Children.* This was a very popular book for children's religious instruction. John Bunyan's 1678 religious parable, *Pilgrim's Progress*, reinforced Puritan beliefs. Originally written for adults, it was quickly condensed for younger readers, who followed with interest the adventures of a man on a pilgrimage to find his way to salvation.

In 1693, John Locke published *Some Thoughts Concerning Education.* In his book, Locke recommended that to encourage reading, a child should be given "some easy pleasant book suited to his capacity."[2] Although Locke rejected the idea of children reading fairy tales, he thought that fables, which usually have a moral, were suitable reading material. Locke recommended *Aesop's Fables* and noted, "If his Aesop has Pictures in it, it will entertain him much the better."[3] In 1702, a publisher identified only as "T. W." issued *A Little Book for Little Children, setting down in a plain and pleasant way, directions for spelling and other remarkable matter. Adorn'd with cuts.* This book was primarily used for children's education.

Two more books written for adults quickly became popular among

John Locke

John Locke may be best known for his political influence. In *Two Treatises of Government*, Locke stressed the rights of citizens and the need for a government to have a system of checks and balances. These ideas greatly influenced the authors of the Declaration of Independence and the U.S. Constitution.

Locke also had strong beliefs about how young people should be educated. His book titled *Some Thoughts Concerning Education* emphasized morals, good manners, and play as important parts of learning. According to him, "They must not be hinder'd from being Children, or from playing, or doing as Children, but from doing ill; all other Liberty is to be allow'd them."[4] Locke also cautioned,

Children should not have any thing like Work, or serious, laid on them; neither their Minds, nor Bodies will bear it. It injures their Healths; and their being forced and tied down to their Books in an age at enmity with all such Restraint, has, I doubt not, been the Reason, why a great many have hated Books and Learning all their Lives after.[5]

children: Daniel Defoe's *Robinson Crusoe* and Jonathan Swift's *Gulliver's Travels.* These books provided exciting stories that awakened children's imaginations. Beginning in 1740, Thomas Boreman created a set of miniature books for children ironically titled *Gigantick Histories.* These books used humor to describe buildings and other sites in London.

In 1744, Newbery wrote and published *A Little Pretty Pocket-Book,* which was the first book truly intended both to inform and entertain children. Following John Locke's advice about making children's books pleasurable, Newbery published books children wanted to read.

Minibooks

In the United States, a miniature book is usually no more than three inches (7.6 cm) in height, width, or thickness. In other countries, miniature books can have dimensions of up to four inches (10.2 cm). Yet, many miniature books are less than three inches (7.6 cm). Easily carried in a pocket, the tiny books cover many subjects, ranging from the Bible to illustrated nursery rhymes.

XV. GOING TO SCHOOL.

These boys and girls are to go to school. What will they do when they get there? They will learn to read, and to write, and to count. You see they have their books with

them. Out of books we learn to read. See, that boy has a slate. He will write on that slate at school. I hope these boys and girls will mind what is said to them at school. They must take pains to learn. The child who does not learn is a dunce.

Before Newbery, books for children were solely instructional.

Newbery's books were popular among children.

NEW KINDS OF BOOKS

In 1744, Newbery published *A Little Pretty Pocket-Book*, which sold more than 10,000 copies before the end of the century. With that publication, Newbery launched a company that would be made famous by its children's books.

Prior to 1744, publishers often produced one book one time with no plans to reprint, or make additional copies. Newbery changed that practice by reprinting *A Little Pretty Pocket-Book* several times. A wise publisher, his first print run of any book was relatively small. Once Newbery saw interest in a product, he printed more of it. He also released new titles on a fairly regular schedule. By doing so, he showed other publishers that children were just as important as adults in the book world.

COURTING CUSTOMERS

To build a customer base for his business, Newbery focused on making his books attractive to children who saw them in his shop window. One way he did this was by gilding the edges of his books. The books clearly differed from the cheap, lackluster look of the chapbooks that children read at the time. His titles were designed to appeal to the interests of children; they also hinted at learning to appeal to parents.

Luckily for Newbery, the standard of living was changing in England. More people were earning higher incomes. Households were beginning to have money to spend on nonessential or luxury items.

Books with gilded pages sold well.

Newbery advertised in ways that let families know that spending money on his books would not be a waste for them or their children.

Many parents wanted their children to grow up to have better lives than they had. They thought Newbery's books would help their children achieve success in life. Newbery understood this attitude and acted on it. His books stressed hard work, good behavior, the value of education, and a belief that a virtuous, hardworking person would be rewarded. He kept his book prices low, which encouraged parents to buy them. Since pocketbooks were in fashion at the time, Newbery deliberately titled his first book *A Little Pretty Pocket-Book* and continued to make more pocket-sized volumes for children.

Soon, there was a growing demand for children's books, especially around the holidays. According to Newbery's biographer, Charles Welsh, Newbery's son Francis wrote of his father:

> [He] was in the full employment of his talents in writing and publishing books of amusement and instruction for children. The call for them was immense, an edition of many thousands being sometimes exhausted during the Christmas holidays.[1]

Advice to Parents

At the beginning of *A Little Pretty Pocket-Book*, Newbery tried to convince parents he cared about their children by suggesting how to raise them:

"Would you have a hardy child, give him common diet only, cloath him thin, let him have good exercise. . . .

Would you have a virtuous son . . . . Take heed what company you intrust [sic] him with, and be sure always to set him a good example yourself.

Would you have a wise son, teach him to reason early. Let him read, and make him understand what he reads. . . ."[2]

MORE AND MORE BOOKS

Newbery followed up the success of his first book with another publication in 1745. It was titled *A Museum for Young Gentlemen and Ladies* or *A Private Tutor for Little Master and Misses, Containing a Variety of useful Subjects.* The book covered the history of Great Britain, the solar system as it was understood at that time, and the manners and customs of the world's nations. Additional sections on the Seven Wonders of the World and the eruption of Mount Vesuvius included many eye-catching illustrations. Between 1745 and 1748, Newbery published a series of educational books that included *Circle of the Sciences: Writing* and *Circle of the Sciences: Arithmetic.* These books have been considered to be the first type of children's encyclopedias.

In 1751, Newbery again started a trend when he published the first English periodical for children, the *Lilliputian Magazine.* The periodical had quite a lengthy alternate title: *The Young Gentleman and Lady's Golden Library. Being An Attempt to mend the World, to render the Society of Man more amiable, and to establish the Plainness, Simplicity, Virtue and Wisdom of the Golden Age, So much celebrated by the Poets and Historians.* Newbery printed only three issues of this magazine. Each issue was filled with riddles, rhymes, jokes, songs, short stories, and recipes. The last issue was published in 1752. Newbery had started a completely new industry and others quickly followed. Between 1752 and 1800, other publishers offered 11 children's magazines.

In 1757, Newbery published *Fables in Verse* under the pseudonym Abraham Aesop. Newbery was able to compile and reword some of the original tales in *Aesop's Fables* because the origins of the fables were unknown. He included fables in his book that he thought would most interest his audience.

Newbery published *Mother Goose's Melody or Sonnets for the Cradle* in 1760. It was an English version of Charles Perrault's 1697 French book, *Tales from the Past with Morals,* subtitled *Tales from My Mother Goose.*

In 1761, Newbery released *The Newtonian System of Philosophy,* also known as *The Philosophy of Tops and Balls,* under

Not Just for Children

Newbery published material for adults too. In 1758, he started *The Universal Chronicle or Weekly Gazette.* The paper featured some of the famous works of Samuel Johnson, including "The Idler," "The Rambler," and "The Lives of the Poets." In 1760, Newbery published the first issue of the *Public Ledger,* featuring "A Citizen of the World," an important work by Oliver Goldsmith. In 1767, Newbery helped finance the publishing of Goldsmith's book *The Vicar of Wakefield,* although Newbery's nephew, Francis, published the book.

the pseudonym Tom Telescope. The book was an introduction to basic physics, astronomy, geography, and natural science. It described the known universe, showed solar and lunar eclipses and how the moon looks through a telescope, and detailed the ideas of Isaac Newton. The book was another popular item for Newbery, selling approximately 30,000 copies before 1800.

In December of 1765, an ad in the *London Chronicle* listed many books Newbery was about to release:

> Mr. Newbery intends to publish the following important volumes, bound and gilt, and hereby invites all his little friends who are good to call for them

Manuscript Mystery

Since Newbery's time, an ongoing controversy has existed about who actually wrote his books. In his day, it was common for authors to use pseudonyms. Some people believe that Oliver Goldsmith, a well-known English author of adult literature and a friend of Newbery, wrote many of the children's books. They point out that Goldsmith sometimes borrowed money from Newbery. This might have been how he repaid the debt.

Other people believe that Newbery is the author of all his own children's books. As evidence, people point to *The Vicar of Wakefield,* in which Goldsmith mentions Newbery as an author of many children's books.

Still others believe two brothers, Giles and Griffith Jones, wrote Newbery's books. Skeptics of Newbery's authorship point out that in 1794, Stephen Jones, the son of Giles, claimed that his father and uncle wrote *The History of Little Goody Two-Shoes*. This has never been proven, so the debate continues.

at the Bible and Sun in St. Paul's Churchyard; but those who are naughty to have none. 1. The Renowned History of Giles Gingerbread; a little boy who lived upon learning. *2.* The Easter Gift; *or the way to be good; a book much wanted. 3.* The Whitsuntide Gift; *or the way to be happy; a book very necessary for all families. 4.* The Valentine Gift; *or how to behave with honour, integrity, and humanity; very useful with a Trading Nation. We are also desired to give notice that there is in the Press, and speedily will be published either by subscription or otherwise, as the Public shall please to determine,* The History of Little Goody Two-Shoes, Otherwise called Mrs. Margery Two-Shoes.[3]

The History of Little Goody Two-Shoes; Otherwise called Mrs. Margery Two-Shoes was released in 1765 and became one of Newbery's most popular books. It was about a virtuous orphan girl who worked hard, got an education, and became a success.

NEWBERY'S MEDICINES

Newbery's medicine business also thrived at 65 St. Paul's Churchyard. Newbery became friendly with Robert James, who was a doctor and a writer.

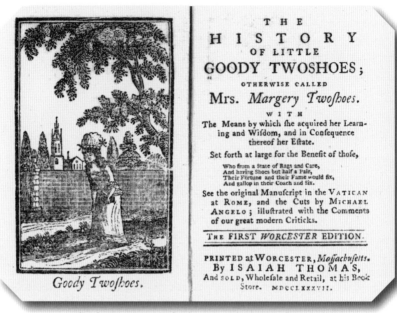

The frontispiece and title page of a later edition of
The History of Little Goody Two-Shoes

From 1743 to 1745, James compiled *Medicinal Dictionary*, a three-volume medical dictionary, and *Pharmacopoeia Universalis*, a listing of medicines and their uses.

Also in 1743, James invented Dr. James's Fever Powder, although he did not receive a patent on it until November 1746. Before it was patented, Newbery and James signed a contract giving the bookseller-merchant the exclusive right to sell the product. Newbery could not make the medicine himself or reveal the secret recipe, but it would be available for his successors if he died. Newbery loaned James money to guarantee the contract that James signed. Of the dozens of remedies Newbery sold at his medicinal shop, Dr. James's Fever Powder was the most popular. Newbery made a great deal of money from that product alone.

Newbery sometimes used his children's books as vehicles to advertise medicines he sold by working the brand names into the plot. For example, in *The History of Little Goody Two-Shoes*, Margery's father was "seized with a violent fever in a place where Dr. James's powder was not to be had, and where he died miserably."[4] The message to readers was that the father would have lived had he been able to take the fever-breaking medicine.

Many people believed in the power of the fever powder—it was

The History of Little Goody Two-Shoes

In *The History of Little Goody Two-Shoes*, poor orphans Margery and Tommy are siblings. Yet, Tommy has two shoes and Margery has only one. A character named Mrs. Smith takes in Margery, and a rich gentleman takes in Tommy, after he orders a pair of shoes made for Margery. When she puts them on, she runs to Mrs. Smith and "stroking down her ragged apron thus cried out, 'Two Shoes, Ma'am, see two Shoes.' And so she behaved to all the people she met, and by that means obtained the name of goody two-shoes."[5]

reportedly used by King George III. In *A Bookseller of the Last Century,* author Horace Walpole is noted as writing,

> *"James' powder is my panacea; that is, it always shall be, for, thank God, I am not apt to have occasion for medicines; but I have such faith in these powders that I believe I should take [them] if the house were on fire."[6]*

The London book business and medicine trade were doing so well, according to Francis Newbery, that his father felt he could no longer spend time on his business in Reading. In the mid-1740s, Newbery allowed others to begin managing the shop. However, he made a deal to receive a portion of the profits.

A Legal Agreement

On February 23, 1746, Dr. Robert James and John Newbery signed an agreement stating that for 21 years, James was "to make his pills for the gout, rheumatism, king's evil, scurfy, and leprosy, and to sell them to J. Newbery."[7] Newbery had exclusive rights to sell the products, but the doctor could dispense them in a different form to his patients. James agreed not to undersell Newbery and to pay Newbery a royalty on any medicines sold abroad.

A LITTLE PRETTY POCKET-BOOK,

Intended for the

Instruction and Amusement

OF

Little Master TOMMY,

AND

Pretty Miss POLLY.

With Two LETTERS from

JACK the GIANT-KILLER;

AS ALSO

A BALL and PINCUSHION;

The Ufe of which will infallibly make TOMMY a good Boy, and POLLY a good Girl.

To which is added,

A LITTLE SONG-BOOK,

BEING

A NEW ATTEMPT to teach CHILDREN the Ufe of the Englifh Alphabet, by Way of Diverfion.

The FIRST *WORCESTER* EDITION.

PRINTED at WORCESTER, *Maffachufett*

The title page of a later edition of A Little Pretty Pocket-Book

Chapter 7

Oliver Goldsmith

Friends and Authors

John Newbery was an ally to authors, helping them with small loans when they needed money. He was an associate of a number of famous English writers, including Oliver Goldsmith, Samuel Johnson, and Christopher Smart. The lives of these men overlapped in their associations with Newbery. They wrote for his publications, often using a pseudonym or writing anonymously, to repay their loans.

OLIVER GOLDSMITH

Newbery became associated with Oliver Goldsmith around 1757. Newbery hired the physician and writer to compile or revise several books and pamphlets. This writing helped Goldsmith pay his bills, since most of his patients were poor and unable to pay him.

Newbery then asked Goldsmith to write for his new periodical, the *Public Ledger*. It debuted on January 12, 1760, featuring the first of Goldsmith's "A Citizen of the World" columns. These were a series of articles about London and English people, supposedly written by a Chinese philosopher named Lien Chi Altangi. They were reprinted in other periodicals and launched Goldsmith's reputation as a writer, even though he used a pseudonym. He soon became friends with others in London's literary and artistic community, including painter Sir Joshua Reynolds and writer Samuel Johnson.

Newbery was not just Goldsmith's employer. He was also his friend. They spent time together in London and Islington, where Newbery lived in Canonbury House. Goldsmith even based a character in *The Vicar of Wakefield* on Newbery, describing him as a busy but generous bookseller:

> *"He was no sooner alighted, but he was in haste to be gone; for he was ever on business of the utmost importance, and was at that time actually compiling materials for the history of one Mr. Thomas Trip."* [1]

It is unknown when Goldsmith wrote *The Vicar of Wakefield,* but it was before 1762, when the book's earnings saved him from debtor's prison. He sent a note to his friend, Samuel Johnson, saying he had not paid his rent for some time and was about to be arrested. Johnson met with Goldsmith and asked if he had any writings that might be sold. Goldsmith gave him the manuscript for a novel, *The Vicar of Wakefield.* Johnson took it to Newbery and sold it, making enough to pay the owed rent.

The book remained unpublished for four years because Newbery was not sure if it would sell well. He finally released it on March 27, 1766, and before the end of May printed a second run of the book.

Demand for the book continued, and Newbery made a good profit from its sales.

SAMUEL JOHNSON

Samuel Johnson is considered one of England's greatest literary figures. He began writing for various periodicals when he moved to London in 1737. His poems, most notably "The Vanity of Human Wishes," launched his career. In 1758, Newbery published the first of Johnson's series of articles called "The Idler" in the *Universal Chronicle, or Weekly Gazette.* The series ran until 1760.

A Witty Friend

In his book *Life of Johnson,* biographer James Boswell writes that Oliver Goldsmith was quite witty but that Johnson and other intellectuals labeled him absurd. According to Goldsmith's biographer, Washington Irving, Johnson once said, "No man is more foolish than Goldsmith when he has not a pen in his hand, or more wise when he has."[2]

To show Goldsmith's wit, Boswell related a story in which Johnson and Goldsmith chatted. Goldsmith announced that he thought he could write good fables because most had a simple structure and the animals in them seldom spoke in character. He cited as an example a fable about little fish that saw birds flying, envied them, and asked Jupiter to change them into birds. Goldsmith explained that the only skill a writer needed was the ability to write dialogue that made fish really sound like fish. Suddenly, Johnson began to shake with laughter, at which point Goldsmith said with a smile, "Why, Dr. Johnson, this is not so easy as you seem to think; for if you were to make little fishes talk, they would talk like whales."[3]

Several of Newbery's friends worked in the publishing industry.

Johnson, like Goldsmith, occasionally borrowed money from Newbery. Like Goldsmith, Johnson wrote about a Newbery-like character, poking a bit of fun at the ever-busy writer, bookseller, pharmacist, and merchant. One of Johnson's "The Idler" articles was about a man named Jack Whirler who was always rushing from place to place. He sat down to eat, took one bite, and then rushed somewhere else where he took the next bite. He visited friends simply to tell them he could not stay and would come back the next day. However, he would do the same on the next day. As Johnson wrote,

> When he enters a house his first declaration is that he cannot sit down; and so short are his visits that he seldom appears to have come for any other reason but to say he must go. [4]

In Johnson's essay, Whirler was swamped with business activities but continued to look for more. He lived an endless cycle of coming up with a new idea, devoting all his energy to making it work, then, when it was almost complete, dropping it to start on a new one that would also never come to fruition.

Johnson may have exaggerated Newbery's behavior to make the

A Home for Friends

Canonbury House, home to Newbery, Goldsmith, Smart, and others, is mentioned in many writings of the seventeenth and eighteenth centuries, including in the following poem:

"See on the distant slope, majestic shews
Old Canonbury's tower, an antient pile,
To various fates assign'd, and where by turns,
Meanness and grandeur have alternate reign'd.
Thither, in later days, have genius fled,
From yonder city, to respire and die.
There the sweet bard of Auburn sat and turn'd
The plaintive moanings of his village dirge;
There learned Chambers treasured lore for men,
And Newbery there his A, B, C's for babes."[5]

Whirler character funnier, but many people saw a connection to Newbery. He was always bustling from place to place, he had several profitable businesses, and he was always coming up with new ideas. However, unlike Whirler, most of Newbery's ideas seem to have been carried out to completion. According to Francis Newbery, his father's reaction to the essay was to jokingly threaten to write a humorous essay about Johnson.

CHRISTOPHER SMART

Newbery's association with poet Christopher Smart began before Smart married Newbery's stepdaughter, Anna Maria Carnan. In 1750, Newbery hired Smart, who had just won the first Seatonian award for religious verse. He wrote many poems for Newbery's Oxford-Cambridge monthly publication, the *Student*. Then Smart worked on Newbery's *Lilliputian Magazine*, which

A Compassionate Friend

Christopher Smart wrote the following epitaph for Newbery's son, John Jr., who died at age 11 after a long illness.

"Henceforth be every
    tender fear supprest,
Or let us weep for joy,
    that he is blest;
From grief to bliss, from
    earth to heav'n
    remov'd,
His mem'ry honour'd, as
    his life belov'd.
That heart o'er which no
    evil e'er had pow'r,
That disposition sickness
    could not sour;
That sense, so oft to riper
    years denied,
That patience heroes
    might have own'd with
    pride!
His painful race undaunt-
    edly he ran,
And in the eleventh
    winter died a man."[6]

was when he met Anna Maria. They married in 1752 and moved into an apartment in Canonbury House that Newbery kept for his writers.

Even with help from friends such as Oliver Goldsmith and David Garrick, Smart was often in debt. Newbery loaned him money and helped when he became ill. Smart died while serving a prison sentence for his debt.

ROBERT JAMES

Robert James was a writer, a doctor, and the inventor of the popular fever powder sold in Newbery's medicine shop. Samuel Johnson may have introduced James to Newbery because the two doctors had gone to grammar school together. In Boswell's *Life of Johnson*, he relates that when James compiled his *Medicinal Dictionary*, Johnson wrote some of the articles and the dedication.

A Lucky Friend

On the way to his first meeting with Newbery, Robert James found a horseshoe on the road. Considering it a sign of good luck, James put the horseshoe in his pocket. The meeting went well, and Newbery became James's agent for the sale of the medicine that made them both a large profit. James credited his success to the horseshoe and used it as a crest on his carriage.

According to Francis Newbery, before James invented his fever powder,

> *He probably might not have attained the eminence he did had it not been for the fortunate discovery of his fever powder; for at his outset, and for several years afterwards, he was in embarrassed circumstances, and gained a livelihood principally by writing for the booksellers. He always expressed the highest regard for Mr John Newbery, declaring that without his friendship and exertions he should not have been able to establish his medicines.[7]*

Newbery's successful business allowed him to help his friends when they needed it. While continuing to publish books, Newbery also continued to foster these friendships.

Samuel Johnson

An illustration in the likeness of John Newbery

LAST YEARS AND LEGACY

John Newbery continued to stay busy throughout his life. After releasing one of his most famous books, *The History of Little Goody Two-Shoes,* in 1765, he continued to write and publish books and run his profitable shop.

In 1767, he released *Tom Thumb's Folio; or, A New Penny Play-Thing for Little Giants.* It contained tiny Tom Thumb's travels, but it also gave readers two fables, "The Fox and the Crow" and "The Dog and the Bee," and a rhyme about Tommy Tag, a virtuous boy:

> *On a pretty bay Nag*
> *Here comes Tommy Tag,*
> *Who ne'er knew Deceit,*
> *Nor wou'd lie, nor wou'd cheat;*
> *As all of you shou'd,*
> *And listen'd, and learn'd, when his Friends did advise,*
> *And so became wealthy, and happy, and wise.*[1]

That same year, Newbery published *Six-Pennyworth of Wit; Or, Little Stories for Little Folks, Of all Denominations* and *The Twelfth-Day Gift; Or The Grand Exhibition,* in which he continued his clever advertising strategies. For example, a line in the book read, "Pulling Mr. Newbery's 'New Year's Gift' out of his pocket, he read."[2] These were the last children's books Newbery published.

NEWBERY REMEMBERED

In the fall of 1767, Newbery became ill. Newbery's friend, Robert James, came to treat him. But despite James's efforts, Newbery did not improve. His son Francis was called home from school at Oxford to be with his family as his father became weaker. Newbery died on December 22, 1767, at the age of 54.

Many people mourned Newbery's passing. Newspapers wrote about the achievements of the man and expressed sadness about his untimely death. At his prior request, Newbery was buried in the churchyard of Waltham St. Lawrence, his hometown.

Shortly after his death, Newbery's books crossed the Atlantic Ocean and began selling in the newly formed United States. Before long, many of his works were reprinted. In some cases, words or phrases were changed to make them more suited to readers in the country. For example, an original Newbery edition might have told children that if they were good, they could ride in "the Lord Mayor's gilt coach."[3] In the U.S. version, the coach would belong to a governor.

A Teaching Man

In the eighteenth century, Newbery's business associate, Benjamin Collins, invented a larger, less expensive substitute for the hornbooks that schoolchildren used. Collins folded cardboard into what he called a battledore. The item looked like a real battledore, or badminton racket. Printed papers were glued on and covered with varnish. As in hornbooks, the alphabet was an important feature, but pictures were included. Each battledore carried a typical Newbery message about the importance of education.

The Will

When Newbery became ill, he worried about what would happen to his businesses. He stipulated in his will who would take over each enterprise:

> the guidance of his step-son, Thomas Carnan, who was still his right-hand man, chiefly in the retail department, and his nephew, Francis, who was more associated with the publishing business. [4]

He left his medicine business solely to his son Francis. Newbery also requested that son Francis, stepson Thomas Carnan, and nephew Francis run the publishing business "for their joint interest and benefit, securing proper provision for his widow and

A Poetic Man

In 1762, Newbery took his son Francis to Oxford, where the boy was to enter Trinity College. That evening, they had dinner with several of Francis's friends who were already in college. Many other students and professors were eating in the same place.

During the course of the meal, a poetry professor took out a striped, pointed cap and popped it on his head. Everyone laughed and asked what the cap meant. He replied that when he was a student at Trinity, he and others started a literary club called "The Jelly Bag Society." The cap was their symbol. The club name and cap, he explained, were inspired by a poem written in 1750 by none other than Newbery in the *Student*. The professor wore the cap in honor of Newbery. After hearing the explanation, Newbery blushed. He said he did not know how anyone knew he had written the poem, because his name was not on it. He thought that people knew because of his distinct writer's style and wit.

his step-daughter, Mrs. Smart, wife of the poet."[5]

However, Newbery's two sons and nephew did not get along. Soon after Newbery's death, nephew Francis set up his own publishing business at No. 20 Ludgate Street, near the corner of St. Paul's Churchyard. He used Newbery as his company name.

Newbery's son Francis and stepson Thomas continued the business in the familiar shop at 65 St. Paul's Churchyard and published books under a new name, T. Carnan and F. Newbery. In the 1772 release of *New History of England*, they inserted the following to alert the public that there was no collaboration between the two firms:

> *London, printed for T. Carnan and F. Newbery, Junior, at No. 65, in St Paul's Church Yard (but not for F. Newbery, at the Corner of Ludgate Street, who has no Share in the late Mr John Newbery's Books for Children).*[6]

Successful on his own, nephew Francis began publishing a periodical in 1767 and continued to

"Stay Passenger, and contemplate
Virtues, which arose on this spot:
Urbanity that adorned society,
Knowledge that instructed it,
Industry, that raised a family to affluence,
Sagacity, that discerned, and
Skill that introduced
The most powerful discovery
In the annals of Medicine."[7]

—*epitaph on Newbery's tomb*

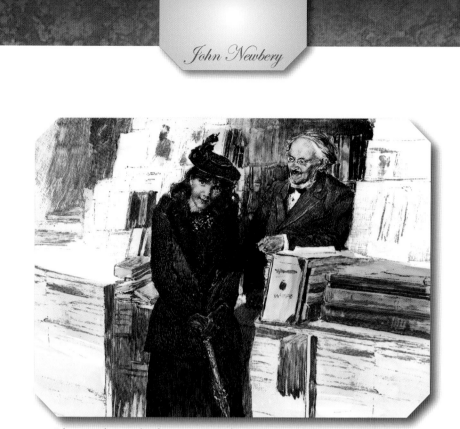

After Newbery's death, young people continued to patronize bookstores to buy Newbery's books.

publish periodicals and books until his death in January 1780. His widow, Elizabeth, hired John Harris as the business manager. In 1802, Elizabeth retired but continued to receive a yearly income until her death in 1821.

The partnership of Newbery's son Francis and stepson Thomas lasted twelve years. Francis had no real business training or experience. He had been studying to be a doctor before his father's death. Thomas Carnan felt that he had not been treated fairly in John Newbery's will. He thought he should have been given a larger share of the business since he was the one who had helped build it. Carnan started publishing books under his own name from the old Newbery bookshop until his death in 1788. Francis then moved to a different location in St. James Churchyard and ran only the medicine business. His successors continued to run the business successfully into the twentieth century.

CARRYING ON THE THEME

Much of children's literature after Newbery's time continued to follow his belief that books should contain a bit of humor. If they did, children would read them. And by reading them, children would learn about the world and the people around them.

After John Harris took over the Newbery publishing business

The Medicine Man

Newbery's old house at the corner of St. Paul's Churchyard was torn down in 1885. Over the fireplace in the shop, workers discovered a panel with the inscription "Newbery's Medicinal Warehouse."[8] There was also a list of more than 30 medicines. It included Dr. James's Powder, Dr. Steer's Oil for Convulsions, and one of the most advertised medicines of the eighteenth century: Dr. Bateman's Drops.

from Elizabeth Newbery, he became an innovator of children's publishing. In 1807, he published *The Butterfly's Ball*, the first in a series of books called *Harris's Cabinet of Amusement and Instruction.* Other titles in the series include *The Peacock at Home* and *The Lion's Masquerade*, which together sold 40,000 copies during their first year published. One particular favorite published by Harris was a book released in 1817 called *Marmaduke Multiply's merry method of making minor mathematicians.* It taught multiplication through interesting illustrations and fun rhymes that helped children memorize multiplication tables.

Harris was succeeded by his son John, who carried on a successful business until 1843. Harris's grandson was even given the name John Newbery Harris.

William Darton also is associated with Newbery's legacy. Darton started his business as a London engraver and printer around 1785. Following Newbery's theme, Darton made specialty books for children, such as *Little Truths better than Great Fables.* Darton formed a partnership with Joseph Harvey. In 1792, they purchased the copyrights to 24 Newbery children's books. In 1792, Darton and Harvey began to republish some of these, starting with *The History*

A Man of Vision

Newbery was a step ahead of others by pioneering advertising strategies for selling books and medicines and by creating new types of books for children. In 1764, Newbery and two other men obtained a patent for a new type of machine for "printing, staining, and colouring silk stuffs, linens, cottons, leather, and paper."[9] This machine would put color on cylinders that would roll over and fill in or stamp color on the material. No one knows whether the machine was ever built.

of Little Goody Two-Shoes, using the old Carnan and Newbery woodcut blocks. By the early 1800s, the partnership of Darton and Harvey was recognized as the leader in the field of children's literature. In 2004, Lawrence Darton, the great-great-great grandson of William Darton, wrote *The Dartons: An Annotated Check-list of Children's Books Issued by Two London Publishing Houses 1787–1876*, which chronicles more than 2,500 Darton children's books.

Newbery's books continued to sell well after his death in 1767.

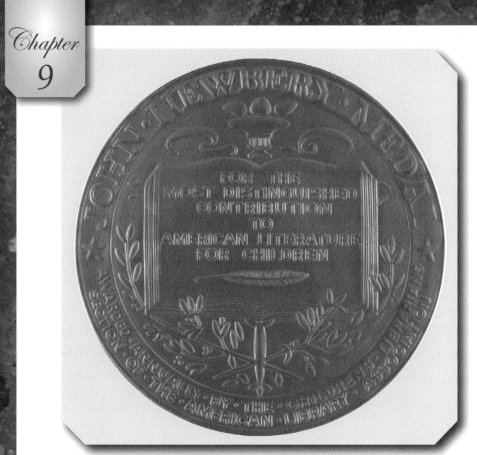

The seal for the Newbery Medal

HONORING NEWBERY

John Newbery has not been forgotten since his death in 1767. More than 150 years later, U.S. publisher Frederic G. Melcher suggested a way of honoring Newbery. In 1921, Melcher presented an idea to the American Library

Association (ALA). He suggested that every year a Newbery award be given for the most distinguished U.S. children's book published during the previous year. The Executive Board of the ALA approved Melcher's idea. The award would serve three purposes:

> *To encourage original creative work in the field of books for children. To emphasize to the public that contributions to the literature for children deserve similar recognition to poetry, plays, or novels. To give those librarians, who make it their life work to serve children's reading interests, an opportunity to encourage good writing in this field.*[1]

Since 1922, the Association for Library Service to Children (ALSC), a division of the ALA, has awarded the Newbery Medal each year. The first medal winner was Hendrik Willem van Loon for *The Story of Mankind*, a history book.

The First Newbery Winner

Hendrik Willem van Loon was a Dutch-American author and illustrator. Born in the Netherlands, he became a U.S. citizen in 1919. While van Loon was researching and writing *The Story of Mankind* in 1921, a children's librarian encouraged him to make the book understandable and entertaining for all ages. When the book won the Newbery Medal, many libraries refused to put it on their shelves because it began with a long discussion of evolution. This concept was considered controversial at the time.

THE MEDAL AND HONORS

The Newbery Sculptor

The Newbery Medal was designed by U.S. sculptor Rene Paul Chambellan. His beautifully carved figures can be seen in many other places, including the Chicago Tribune Building, the fountains at New York's Rockefeller Center, and the bronze doors of the Davidson County Courthouse in Nashville, Tennessee. In 1937, he designed the Caldecott Medal, another award for children's books.

The Newbery Medal became the world's first children's book award. A famous sculptor designed the medal, which has an engraving on the front in a likeness of Newbery with children. The title of the winning book and the date the honor was received appear on the back of each medal. Although there are several other awards for young people's literature, the Newbery Medal remains the best-known and most discussed children's book award.

Winning a Newbery Medal can change an author's life, professionally and financially. There is no cash prize with the medal, but library and bookstore shelves are set aside specifically for Newbery Medal winners. Plus, additional books and previously written books by the winning author usually advertise on their covers that the author is a winner of the Newbery Medal. By winning the medal, the sales of an author's books can increase dramatically, and every book sale means a royalty for the writer. Shortly after *Good Masters! Sweet Ladies!* won the Newbery in 2008, sales of the book jumped from more than eight-thousandth place to seventeenth in book sales on Amazon.com. After the Newbery Medal committee's announcement in 2006 that *Criss Cross* had won, it jumped from approximately three-hundred-thousandth place to twenty-fifth in less than 12 hours.

CHOOSING A NEWBERY WINNER

Many good children's books are written each year, which means the Newbery Award committee has a challenging job to select the winner. The committee consists of 15 members of the ALSC, a group that includes librarians, parents, authors, booksellers, and

The Book Man

Frederic G. Melcher spent his lifetime championing books. At 16, he started working in a Massachusetts bookstore and then moved to Indiana to manage a bookstore. Melcher later relocated to New York and became coeditor of *Publisher's Weekly* in 1918. He always looked for ways to celebrate books and encourage reading, including special editions of his publication devoted to children's literature. In 1919, he cofounded Children's Book Week. Melcher felt Book Week was important because it allowed people across the nation to focus on children's reading. National Children's Book Week is still celebrated each year.

When Melcher met with children's librarians at the 1921 ALA convention, he proposed the Newbery Medal as a way to encourage and celebrate children's literature. In 1937, Melcher suggested a second medal to honor children's books. The Caldecott Medal is given annually for the most distinguished picture book for children.

Cynthia Richey, president of the ALSC, awarded Kate DiCamillo the 2004 Newbery Medal for The Tale of Despereaux.

publishers. Seven members and the committee chair are elected by ballot. The president of the ALSC appoints the remaining seven members to assure ethnic, gender, professional, and geographic balance.

From approximately 5,000 children's books published each year in the United States, the committee identifies approximately 100 books to consider as serious candidates for the award. Choices are narrowed down further during the year to approximately 35 by the time the committee votes for one winner. The members choose a few books as honor books. The front cover of every medal-winning or honor book has a label identifying it as a Newbery recipient.

To be considered for a Newbery Medal, a book can be fiction, nonfiction, or poetry. A book must be original and published in English, and the author must be a citizen or resident of the United States. A book also must show an understanding of the audience, which consists of children up to age 14.

APPEALING TO READERS

A note in the Newbery Medal criteria also states, "The committee should keep in mind that the award is for literary quality and quality presentation for children. The award is not for [educational] intent or for popularity."[2] Yet, some people say that John Newbery always linked learning and enjoyment, knowing that if children liked his books, they would read more. Some books are widely popular but never win the Newbery Medal. A few, however, have been named as honor books. These include *Charlotte's Web*,

which won in 1953, and Laura Ingalls
Wilder's *Little House* books, which won
five times from 1938 to 1944.

Anita Silvey is an expert in
children's literature. In an article
published in the October 2008 *School
Library Journal,* she questioned whether
the Newbery Medal had lost some
of its appeal. She surveyed more
than 100 librarians, teachers, and
booksellers in 15 states and found
that many were disappointed with
recent Newbery winners.

People told Silvey the books did
not connect with most young readers
and often turned them off because
of the depressing content. Books
about death, injustice, loss, and
impossible odds have been winners
over the years. Recent winners have
covered new social issues such as
homelessness, the absence of one
or both parents, and the mental
challenges of autism. Some experts
say life is tough and children's

Two-time Winners

Five authors have won the
Newbery Medal twice.
• E. L. Konigsburg: *From
the Mixed-Up Files of
Mrs. Basil E. Frankweiler,*
1997; *The View from Sat-
urday,* 1968
• Joseph   Krumgold:
. . . *And Now Miguel,*
1954; *Onion John,* 1960
• Lois Lowry: *Number
the Stars,* 1990; *The Giver,*
1994
• Katherine   Paterson:
Bridge to Terabithia, 1978;
Jacob Have I Loved, 1981
• Elizabeth   George
Speare: *The Witch of
Blackbird Pond,* 1959;
The Bronze Bow, 1962

literature reflects the times. But school librarians reported that they did not have money to spend on books that children would not find interesting to read.

One person who was interviewed for the article suggested that the Newbery committee appeared "to be hunting for a special book—one with only a few readers, rather than a universal book."[3] A member of the 1953 Newbery Medal committee that chose *The Secret of the Andes* over *Charlotte's Web* said she preferred the former because she had not seen any good books about South America.

Many people have suggested that the committee should change its criteria and look at a book's appeal to a large audience of children. Others suggest that since the Newbery Medal honors the publisher who created materials specifically for the education and amusement of children, children themselves

Newbery Films

Many Newbery award books have been made into movies and include:
- *Island of the Blue Dolphins* (1961); movie released 1964
- *A Wrinkle in Time* (1963); movie released 2003
- *Sounder* (1970); movie released 1972
- *Bridge to Terabithia* (1978); movie released 2007
- *Sarah, Plain and Tall* (1986); movie released 1991
- *Shiloh* (1992); movie released 1996
- *Holes* (1999); movie released 2003
- *The Tale of Despereaux* (2004); movie released 2008

should have a say in choosing the winner. In some communities, schools already encourage students to read the books that are possible candidates for the medal, discuss them, and vote for a winner. The students' results are sent to that year's new committee chair and listed on the ALSC Web site. Once the winner is chosen, students learn whether their selections matched the committee's.

Recently, some people believe the committee is finally beginning to look at what children like to read. *The Graveyard Book* was announced as the 2009 Newbery winner. Before the announcement, it had been on the *New York Times* best-seller list for children's books for 15 weeks and had sold 71,000 copies. It was a book that appealed to many children, just like the books of the legendary John Newbery. ⁓

Young readers today can thank Newbery for popularizing
children's literature.

TIMELINE

1713	1730	ca. 1734
John Newbery is born in July in Waltham St. Lawrence, England.	Newbery is apprenticed to William Ayres, publisher of the *Reading Mercury*.	William Carnan takes over the *Reading Mercury*. Carnan then teaches Newbery the skills of a printer and a merchant.

1740	1741	1742
Newbery publishes his first books for adults.	Newbery opens a printing business and a warehouse for haberdashery supplies. He expands his medicine business.	Newbery creates the Newbery Circulating Library in Reading, England.

1737	1739	1739
William Carnan dies. He wills his business to his brother and to Newbery.	Newbery marries Mary Carnan and becomes stepfather to her three children.	Newbery becomes publisher of the *Reading Mercury*. Charles Micklewright becomes his partner.

1744	1744	1745
Newbery opens a shop and warehouse in London.	Newbery writes and publishes *A Little Pretty Pocket-Book* to inform and entertain children.	Newbery moves his family to London and opens the Bible and Sun at St. Paul's Churchyard.

LITTLE PRETTY
OCKET-BOOK,
INTENDED FOR THE
INSTRUCTION and AMUSEMENT
OF
LITTLE MASTER TOMMY,
AND
PRETTY MISS POLLY.
With Two LETTERS from
JACK the GIANT-KILLER;
AS ALSO
A BALL and PINCUSHION;
The Use of which will infallibly make TOMMY
a good Boy, and POLLY a good Girl.
To which is added,
LITTLE SONG-BOO

TIMELINE

1746

Newbery signs a
contract for the
exclusive right to sell
Dr. James's
Fever Powder.

1746

Newbery and
Benjamin Collins
print Collins's
battledore, a
cardboard schoolbook
for teaching children.

1751

Newbery publishes
the first children's
periodical, the
Lilliputian Magazine.

1761

Using the name
Tom Telescope,
Newbery writes
*The Newtonian
System of Philosophy.*

1765

Newbery publishes
*The History of Little
Goody Two-Shoes.*

1757	1758	1760
Using the name Abraham Aesop, Newbery publishes *Fables in Verse.*	Newbery starts a newspaper that features Samuel Johnson's series "The Idler."	Newbery publishes *Mother Goose's Melody or Sonnets for the Cradle* and the first issue of the *Public Ledger* newspaper.

1767	1922
Newbery releases his last books for children. He dies on December 22.	The first Newbery Medal is awarded to Hendrik Willem van Loon for *The Story of Mankind.*

Essential Facts

Date of Birth

July 1713

Place of Birth

Waltham St. Lawrence, England

Date of Death

December 22, 1767

Known Parent

Robert Newbery

Education

School in Waltham St. Lawrence; apprenticeship under William Ayres in Reading, England

Marriage

Mary Carnan (1739)

Children

John (stepson), Thomas (stepson), Anna Maria (stepdaughter), Mary, John, and Francis

CAREER HIGHLIGHTS

Newbery established children's books as a distinct genre of literature. He was a newspaper and book publisher and also a merchant of medicines in England.

SOCIETAL CONTRIBUTION

Newbery paved the way for a new type of children's books. His belief that children should be able to read entertaining material was groundbreaking.

RESIDENCES

Waltham St. Lawrence, England; Reading, England; London, England

CONFLICTS

Newbery's belief that children should have entertaining reading material was at odds with his contemporaries' beliefs that children's reading material should be solely educational and religiously instructive.

QUOTE

"John Newbery has often been credited with originating the publication of children's books; in reality, though, his role was even more important: he began the serious business of publishing for children."—*Margaret Kinnell,* Children's Literature: An Illustrated History, 1995

ADDITIONAL RESOURCES

SELECT BIBLIOGRAPHY

Hunt, Peter, ed. *Children's Literature: An Illustrated History.* Oxford: Oxford UP, 1995.

Townsend, John Rowe. *John Newbery and His Books: Trade and Plumb-Cake for Ever, Huzza!* Metuchen, NJ: Scarecrow, 1994.

Townsend, John Rowe. *Written for Children: An Outline of English-Language Children's Literature.* Philadelphia, PA: Lippincott, 1974.

Welsh, Charles. *A Bookseller of the Last Century: Being Some Account of the Life of John Newbery, and of the Books he Published, with a Notice of the later Newberys.* London: Griffith, Farran, Okeden & Welsh, 1885.

FURTHER READING

Blackstock, Josephine. *Songs for Sixpence: A Story About John Newbery.* New York: Follett, 1955.

Dalgliesh, Alice. *A Book for Jennifer: A Story of London Children in the Eighteenth Century and of Mr. Newbery's Juvenile Library.* New York: Charles Scribner's Sons, 1952.

Roberts, Russell. *John Newbery and the Story of the Newbery Medal.* Hockessin, DE: Mitchell Lane, 2004.

WEB LINKS

To learn more about John Newbery, visit ABDO Publishing Company online at **www.abdopublishing.com**. Web sites about John Newbery are featured on our Book Links page. These links are routinely monitored and updated to provide the most current information available.

Places to Visit

Baldwin Library of Historical Children's Literature
University of Florida Department of Special Collections,
George A. Smathers Libraries
Gainesville, FL 32611
352-273-2757
www.uflib.ufl.edu/spec/baldwin/baldwin.html
This library contains more than 100,000 volumes of children's
literature published from the mid-1600s through 2007 in Great
Britain and the United States.

Children's Literature Center, Library of Congress
101 Independence Avenue Southeast, Thomas Jefferson Building,
LJ 129
Washington, DC 20540-4620
202-707-5535
www.loc.gov/rr/child/
The Children's Literature Center is used by people from around
the world who study and produce all types of children's literature.

Lilly Library
Indiana University, 1200 East Seventh Street
Bloomington, IN 47405
47405-5500
812-855-2452
www.indiana.edu/~liblilly/overview/lit_child.shtml
The children's literature collection at the Lilly Library holds
approximately 10,000 books, including the oldest known copy of
the 1763 edition of *A Little Pretty Pocket-Book* and a copy of *The History of
Little Goody Two-Shoes*.

GLOSSARY

apprentice
Someone who is learning a trade or art by practical experience or on-the-job training under the guidance of a skilled professional.

broadside
A large sheet of paper with an illustration and a line or two of text.

chapbook
A small, short book filled with short stories, jokes, and recipes.

circulation
The average number of copies a publication sells in a period of time.

elixir
A medicinal mixture.

epitaph
An inscription on a gravestone in memory of the person buried there.

frontispiece
An illustration preceding a title page of a book.

gilded
Covered with a thin layer of gold.

haberdashery
A shop that sells items for sewing such as needles, pins, and ribbons.

hornbook
A kind of first reader for schoolchildren.

legacy
How someone will be remembered for what he or she did or will pass on to future generations.

periodical
A publication that is published on a schedule with a fixed time between issues, such as daily, weekly, monthly, or yearly.

pharmacist
>   A person who prepares, mixes, and dispenses medical drugs.

philosophy
>   The most basic beliefs and attitudes of an individual or a group.

primer
>   A small book used to teach children to read.

print run
>   The number of copies of a publication that are printed in one set.

pseudonym
>   A fictitious name or pen name.

publisher
>   A person or a company whose business is to print and sell the work of an author.

readership
>   A publication's group of readers.

royalty
>   A payment to a person for each copy of an item sold.

virtuous
>   Characteristic of someone who always tries to do the right thing and has good moral values.

Source Notes

Chapter 1. Books for Children

1. John Rowe Townsend. *John Newbery and His Books: Trade and Plumb-Cake for Ever, Huzza!* Metuchen, NJ: Scarecrow, 1994. 7.
2. Ibid.
3. Charles Welsh. *A Bookseller of the Last Century: Being Some Account of the Life of John Newbery, and of the Books He Published, with a Notice of the Later Newberys.* London: Griffith, Farran, Okeden & Welsh, 1885. 109.
4. Oliver Goldsmith. *The Vicar of Wakefield.* London: Macmillan, 1910. 151.
5. Peter Hunt, ed. *Children's Literature: An Illustrated History.* Oxford: Oxford UP, 1995. 34.
6. Charles Welsh. *A Bookseller of the Last Century: Being Some Account of the Life of John Newbery, and of the Books He Published, with a Notice of the Later Newberys.* London: Griffith, Farran, Okeden & Welsh, 1885. 293.
7. Ibid. 111.
8. Ibid. 110.
9. Ibid. 109.
10. Bernice E. Leary. "Milestones in Children's Books." *Books at Iowa.* April 1970. The University of Iowa Libraries: Special Collections and University Archives. 12 Apr. 2009. <http://www.lib.uiowa.edu/spec-coll/bai/leary.htm>.

Chapter 2. A Country Boy

1. Charles Welsh. *A Bookseller of the Last Century: Being Some Account of the Life of John Newbery, and of the Books He Published, with a Notice of the Later Newberys.* London: Griffith, Farran, Okeden & Welsh, 1885. 5.
2. Ibid.

Chapter 3. Taking Care of Business

1. R. M. Wiles. *The Freshest Advices: Early Provincial Newspapers in England.* Columbus: Ohio State UP, 1965. 153.
2. Charles Welsh. *A Bookseller of the Last Century: Being Some Account of the Life of John Newbery, and of the Books He Published, with a Notice of the Later Newberys.* London: Griffith, Farran, Okeden & Welsh, 1885. 11.
3. Ibid. 12–13.
4. Ibid. 9.

Chapter 4. Off to London

1. Samuel Johnson. *In Imitation of the Third Satire of Juvenal Online.* "London: A Poem." 1738. 16 Mar. 2009 <http://andromeda. rutgers.edu/~jlynch/Texts/london.html>.

2. James Boswell. *The Life of Samuel Johnson.* New York: Modern Library, 1931. 733.

Chapter 5. Children's Literature before Newbery

1. C. M. Hewins. "The History of Children's Books." *Atlantic Monthly Online.* Jan. 1888. 16 Mar. 2009 <http://www.theatlantic.com/ doc/188801/childrens-books>.

2. John Locke. *Some Thoughts Concerning Education.* Cambridge: Cambridge UP, 1895. 133.

3. Ibid. 133.

4. Ibid. 45.

5. Ibid. 131.

Chapter 6. New Kinds of Books

1. Charles Welsh. *A Bookseller of the Last Century: Being Some Account of the Life of John Newbery, and of the Books He Published, with a Notice of the Later Newberys.* London: Griffith, Farran, Okeden & Welsh, 1885. 22–23.

2. John Rowe Townsend. *John Newbery and His Books: Trade and Plumb-Cake for Ever, Huzza!* Metuchen, NJ: Scarecrow, 1994. 4–6.

3. C. M. Hewins. "The History of Children's Books." *Atlantic Monthly Online.* Jan. 1888. 16 Mar. 2009 < http://www.theatlantic. com/doc/188801/childrens-books>.

4. Charlotte Mary Yonge. *A Storehouse of Stories.* London: Macmillan, 1890. 70.

5. Ibid. 71.

6. Charles Welsh. *A Bookseller of the Last Century: Being Some Account of the Life of John Newbery, and of the Books He Published, with a Notice of the Later Newberys.* London: Griffith, Farran, Okeden & Welsh, 1885. 26.

7. Ibid. 21.

Source Notes Continued

Chapter 7. Friends and Authors

1. Oliver Goldsmith. *The Vicar of Wakefield*. London: Macmillan, 1910. 151.
2. Washington Irving. *Oliver Goldsmith: A Biography*. New York: Putnam, 1864. 203.
3. James Boswell. *The Life of Samuel Johnson*. London: Baldwin and Son, 1799. 230.
4. John Rowe Townsend. *John Newbery and His Books: Trade and Plumb-Cake for Ever, Huzza!* Metuchen, NJ: Scarecrow. 1994. 27.
5. Charles Welsh. *A Bookseller of the Last Century: Being Some Account of the Life of John Newbery, and of the Books He Published, with a Notice of the Later Newberys*. London: Griffith, Farran, Okeden & Welsh, 1885. 47.
6. Ibid. 7–8.
7. Ibid. 24–25.

Chapter 8. Last Years and Legacy

1. *Tom Thumb's Folio; or, A New Penny Play-Thing for Little Giants*. London: Carnan and Newbery, 1779. 31.
2. Charles Welsh. *A Bookseller of the Last Century: Being Some Account of the Life of John Newbery, and of the Books He Published, with a Notice of the Later Newberys*. London: Griffith, Farran, Okeden & Welsh, 1885. 110.
3. C. M. Hewins. "The History of Children's Books." *Atlantic Monthly Online*. Jan. 1888. 13 Apr. 2009 <http://www.theatlantic.com/issues/1888jan/hewins.htm>.
4. Charles Welsh. *A Bookseller of the Last Century: Being Some Account of the Life of John Newbery, and of the Books He Published, with a Notice of the Later Newberys*. London: Griffith, Farran, Okeden & Welsh, 1885. 70.
5. Ibid. 82.
6. Ibid. 83.
7. Ibid. 71.
8. Ibid. 22.
9. Ibid. 69.

Chapter 9. Honoring Newbery
1. "About the Newbery Medal." *ALA.org.* American Library Association. 2009. 13 Apr. 2009 <http://www.ala.org/ala/mgrps/divs/alsc/awardsgrants/bookmedia/newberymedal/aboutnewbery/aboutnewbery.cfm>.
2. "Terms and Criteria: John Newbery Medal." *ALA.org.* American Library Association. 2009. 20 Apr. 2009 <http://www.ala.org/ala/mgrps/divs/alsc/awardsgrants/bookmedia/newberymedal/newberyterms/newberyterms.cfm>.
3. Anita Silvey. "Has the Newbery Lost Its Way?" *School Library Journal.* 1 Oct. 2008. 20 Apr. 2009 <http://www.schoollibraryjournal.com/article/CA6600688.html>.

INDEX

ABOUT THE AUTHOR

Shirley Consodine Granahan writes books from her home near New York City, where she lives with her daughter and granddaughter. Before beginning her career as an author, Granahan was a classroom teacher and a professional singer, actress, and storyteller. She is the recipient of nine EdPress Awards and a Bicentennial Award from the U.S. government for her book on the U.S. Constitution.

PHOTO CREDITS